Are You a Ten? The Ten Characteristics of a Servant Leader

Are You a Ten? The Ten Characteristics of a Servant Leader

Barbara Baggerly-Hinojosa

ISBN 978-0-557-80080-3

Acknowledgements

I want to thank my dear husband, C.A., for his many hours of listening to me talk on and on and on about this project. He is the one that always lets me dream big dreams but pulls me gently down to reality when the dreams get so big I can't see straight.

I also want to thank my three favorite people in the world – Benjamin, Ana Alicia, and Isaac. My three children are what I wake up for in the morning and why I am so tired in the evening. I love them all dearly.

Of course, I have to thank my parents, Marty and Ronnie Baggerly. Mom and Dad provided me a loving home where we girls were taught that we could be anything we wanted in life. To my sister, Susan, I thank you for always being my number one cheerleader.

To my inlaws, Claudio and Belinda Hinojosa, I thank you and love you for your everlasting support.

To my entire OLLU family, thank you for all that you have taught me. I will never forget your support and friendship.

Additional thanks goes to my childhood friend LaShawn Brown Sithole for her encouragement, wisdom, and sympathetic ear.

This book is dedicated to my real life role model and perfect example of a Servant Leader – my grandmother, Norma Jean Lipscomb.

Preface

In 1977, Robert K. Greenleaf coined the term, Servant Leadership to describe a person who desired to serve first and foremost. Greenleaf described a kind of leadership that is primarily motivated by a deep desire to help others.

"It begins with the natural feeling that one wants to serve. Then conscious choice brings one to aspire to lead. This is sharply different from the person who is leader first. The difference manifests itself in the care taken by the servant first to make sure that other people's highest priority needs are being served." --Robert K. Greenleaf

Table of Contents

Chapter 1

Listening- Are You a Good Listener?

Week 1 – Listening

An old Italian proverb says, "From listening comes wisdom, from speaking comes repentance." Listening begins with attention and the search for understanding. Why is there so little listening? In the face of a difficult situation, the usual leader tends to react by trying to find someone else to blame. A true servant leader will listen first because true listening builds strength in others. As Robert Greenleaf said, "In saying what I have in mind will I really improve the silence?" We need to overcome the tendency to speak all the time. Silence is a good thing and we must not be afraid of it.

Listening can be described as an attitude toward other people. You may think that you are a good listener, but do the people around you disagree? Has anyone ever looked at you with a disappointed expression and said, "Are you listening to me?" My bet is that has happened to you at least once. It has happened to me. Well, don't be too discouraged, collectively, we are poor listeners. In fact, according to the International Listening Association we only retain about half of what we hear immediately after we hear it, and only about 20% beyond that. Those are not good percentages, are they? Despite these disappointing stats, listening is one of the most important parts of successful communication. Maybe we just get caught up in the sound of our own voices and forget to be quiet and hear what others are saying.

Imagine if we were all able to boost our ability to listen so that we retained 75% of what we heard immediately after hearing it and 50% long term? Wow, think about that! The implications of this more effective listening would be tremendous because we would spend less time trying to recall what we can't remember. The quality of our work would improve, we would likely get into fewer arguments, and our relationships would be stronger. Better listening habits will allow us to have more empathy and compassion for others. Researchers have found that the average individual spends considerably more time each day in listening that in speaking, writing, or reading. Therefore, improving your listening skills is a very important communicative task. Did you know that we devote about 40 or 45 percent of our working hours to listening? And did you know that, if you have not taken steps to improve this skill, you listen at only 25 percent efficiency? Putting these thoughts together, do you feel comfortable knowing that you earn 40 percent or more of your pay while listening at 25 percent efficiency? Perhaps acting on the information shared in this chapter will improve your listening skill to above the average in listening efficiency. Tests have shown that we can significantly raise the level of our listening performance by a small amount of study and practice. Listening is typically thought of as a passive duty. In fact, the opposite is really true. Intensive listening should leave you feeling quite tired after a speaker has finished saying what they had to say.

It takes a lot of concentration and determination to be an active listener. Old habits are hard to break, and if your listening habits are as many people's are, then there's a lot of habit breaking to do. Be deliberate with your listening and remind yourself constantly that your goal is to truly hear what the other person is saying. Set aside all other thoughts and behaviors and concentrate on the message. Ask questions, reflect, and paraphrase to ensure you understand the message. If you don't, then you'll find that what someone says to you and what you hear can be amazingly different!

That brings us to the question, how can we do a better job at listening? Let's face it, being a good listener is not as easy as it sounds. We've all drifted off into our own thoughts when we were supposed to be paying attention to what someone else was saying. Maybe it's because the subject matter is boring or the person speaking is not very interesting. Or, perhaps we are distracted by some personal matters. I hope the tips discussed in this chapter can help improve your listening skills. Start using active listening today to become a better communicator and improve your workplace productivity and relationships. The skill of listening is the first characteristic in the ten characteristics of a servant leader.

So, what do you say, let's work on becoming a better listener. The following five daily exercises will help you become a more effective listener as you travel on your road to become a more effective Servant Leader.

<u>Monday – Lesson #1 – Pay Attention!</u>

It is the beginning of the week and the beginning of our exercise to become a better listener. As you go about your day today, be conscious of your ability to pay attention to those speaking to you. As you practice the art of listening, use the following as a checklist. At the end of the day, place a check mark next to each item that you completed. At the end of the week, you will reflect on all the steps you took to promote your listening skills.

Listen more than you talk	
Stay focused on what the other person is saying – not on what you're going to say next	
Don't plan a story while the person is still talking	
Never finish another person's sentence	
Look at the speaker directly	
Put aside distracting thoughts	
Refrain from side conversations when listening in a group setting	
Face your speaker	
Make eye contact	
Stop doing other things	
Pay attention to the speaker's words	
Pay attention to nonverbal clues such as speaker's facial expressions and tone of voice	

Tuesday – Lesson #2 – Provide Feedback

O.k., Day 2 is ahead and you have now had some practice with paying attention. Now, you need to practice providing feedback. Feedback will allow your speaker to speak freely to you. As you did yesterday, please take the time at the end of the day today to reflect on your experiences and place a check mark on the following items that you practiced. As a reminder, at the end of the week, you will review all the strategies you practiced this week in order to develop your listening skills more effectively. Have fun!

Focus on using body language	
Make eye contact	
Uncross your arms	
Turn your shoulders so that you are facing the speaker	
Create memory triggers to assist your recall	
Nod occasionally	
Smile and use other facial expressions	
Note your posture and make sure it is open and inviting	
Encourage the speaker to continue with small verbal comments like, "yes," and "uh huh"	

Wednesday – Lesson #3 – Defer Judgment

Day three and you are getting the hang of things. You have practiced paying attention and providing feedback, now time for the hard stuff. In order to be a good listener you must be able to not judge the speaker. As we all know, it is human nature for us to judge others so this lesson will take some practice. So, practice we will do. As usual, place a check mark next to the items that you practiced today then at the end of the week you will reflect on what you learned and what you experienced. Good luck and remember you will be a much better listener and leader for trying these techniques.

Empathize – put yourself in the speaker's shoes so that you get a deeper understanding of the speaker's feelings	
Be open minded	
Allow the speaker to finish	
Don't interrupt with counter-arguments	
Share in the speaker's emotions and feelings	
Validate the speaker	
Try to rid yourself of biases or preconceptions that can distort what you hear or your understanding of it	

Thursday – Lesson #4 – Respond Appropriately

You made it through your hardest day yesterday. Today's lesson is on how to respond appropriately. To be an effective listener, you must be an active listener. In order to be an active listener, you must make sure that the speaker knows that you are following along with the conversation. Practice the following skills and check off the ones you try in real life situations. Tomorrow is reflecting day so try and practice as many of these as you can. You are almost done with the first week of activities. I just know you are feeling accomplished about now, aren't you?

Resist the urge to dominate the conversation	
Don't interrupt	
Stop doing other things	
Reflect on what the speaker has said by paraphrasing	
Ask questions to clarify certain points	
Summarize the speaker's comments periodically	
Be candid, open, and honest in your responses	
Assert your opinions respectfully	
Encourage the speaker with an understanding nod or say, "I see" or "that makes sense."	
Ask open ended questions to promote further discussion	
Don't say, "I told you so" or "I knew that."	
Eliminate any attempt to try to impress the speaker and show how smart and funny you are.	

Friday – Lesson #5 – Exercise your Mind

You made it! It is Friday and you have had the opportunity to practice a variety of skills that will assist you in your quest to become a better listener and an excellent Servant Leader. You worked on paying attention, providing feedback, deferring judgment, and responding appropriately. Today, you will exercise your mind. Take this day to reflect on Lessons #1 - #5 and use this time to write down some comments on which lessons you feel were hard and which lessons you feel were easy.

Realize that listening is hard work	
Recognize your own biases	
Develop an appetite for hearing a variety of presentations	
Prepare to listen by having an open mind and a positive mental attitude	

Journal

Chapter 2

Empathy- Can You Really Walk in Someone Else's Shoes?

Week 2 – Empathy

Very simply put, empathy means we can walk in someone else's shoes (not literally, of course). Actually, we can define empathy as the sharing of another person's feelings. Researchers have found that when we see other people hurting, our brains respond in a characteristic way. Our brain reacts to pain in others the same way it reacts to pain in ourselves.

As stated by Robert Greenleaf, the servant leader must always accept and empathize with another person and should never reject others. Even though the servant as leader always empathizes and accepts the person, the effective servant leader refuses to accept some of the person's effort or performance as good enough. For a great leader, especially a Servant Leader, showing empathy and acceptance of others is essential to the growth and development of the people who live and work with them. The truth is, anybody can lead perfect people. However, I haven't met a perfect person yet, have you? Even though the work performance of others may be judged critically, people grow taller and perform their work tasks better when those who lead them empathize and accept them.

Empathy is a vehicle for effective understanding, communication, and relationships. It is essential to find the solutions to problems that are so prevalent in today's economic world. Empathy is essential in handling complaints and retaining customers. The reality is, in today's world, we must be more effective communicators if we want to be successful in business and in life. Empathy is essential in handling complaints, retaining customers, building relationships, and leading others at home and in the workplace. Most modern gurus in the areas of communications, management, and self-development refer in one way or another to the importance of empathy. We need to learn how to really understand another person's feelings and emotions in order to promote professional and personal growth in ourselves and in others.

Showing empathy to your colleagues and family will help build trust because a leader who can empathize with others can also be trusted. Acquiring empathy is about being in tune with who you are as a person. The good news is, empathy involved skills and social beliefs, most of which can be learned. I believe that people working on and developing their empathy skills can ultimately end some of the human suffering that happens on a daily basis in our world...it is THAT important and powerful!

Empathy is not an easy skill to learn and it is definitely not and easy skill to teach. But, with some practice and patience (and yes, prayer), you will be able to refine and develop your empathy skills this week by working on the following daily suggestions. Keep in mind that by becoming more empathetic, you are one step closer to becoming a more effective Servant Leader. We all should be more conscious of how we relate to others because this world could use a few more Servant Leaders, don't you agree?

Monday – Lesson #1 – Reflect on Your Own Feelings and Distinguish Them From the Feelings of Others

It is the beginning of a new week and the beginning of our exercise to become more empathetic. Empathy is not such an easy skill to learn. But, with some practice and patience, you will be able to refine your empathy skills this week. Keep in mind that becoming more empathetic is one step toward becoming a more effective Servant Leader. As you go about your day today, be conscious of how you relate to others' feelings. As you practice the art of empathizing, use the following as a checklist. At the end of the day, place a check mark next to each item that you completed. At the end of the week, you will reflect on all the steps you took to promote your empathy skills.

Work on self-awareness – recognize your own needs	
Take another person's perspective	
Regulate your own emotional response…don't overreact to a situation	
Think about your own moral and political views	
Acknowledge, identify, and accept your feelings	

Tuesday – Lesson #2 – Imagine the Perspective of Another Person

Today, you will practice imagining the perspective of others. This skill takes some practice so be sure to try all the tips listed. As you did yesterday, please take the time at the end of the day today to reflect on your experiences and place a check mark on the following items that you practiced. At the end of the week, you will get the chance to review all the strategies you practiced this week in order to develop your empathy skills.

Seize opportunities today to model sympathetic feelings for other people	
Discover what you have in common with other people from other cultures and backgrounds	
Make a face while trying to imagine how someone else feels	
Become familiar with other people	
Identify similarities between yourself and others	
Read or watch stories for opportunities to practice perspective-taking skills – What do the characters think, believe, want, or feel? And how do we know it?	
Have an open door policy where your followers can feel welcome to talk about their experiences, both positive and negative	
Practice your listening skills (Lesson #1)	
Place yourself in the position of the other person	
Cultivate compassion	

Wednesday – Lesson #3 – Bounce Back from Negative Emotions!

It is day three and I'm sure you are getting the hang of things. You have practiced reflecting on your feelings and others, as well as imagining the perspective of others. In order to empathize you must be able to bounce back from negative emotions. It is human nature for us to experience these negative emotions and let them take over, so this lesson will take some practice. As usual, place a check mark next to the items that you practiced today then at the end of the week you will reflect on what you learned and what you experienced.

Keep your emotions under control by using active listening skills	
Think before you act	
Don't let yourself dwell on the negative	
Find something positive about the situation	
Be thankful today for all that is good and right in your world	
Journal about the positive things that are happening around you	

Thursday – Lesson #4 – Establish Rapport with Others

Today's lesson is on how to establish rapport with others. This week you are find out that to be a leader who serves, you must have empathy. In order to have empathy, you must make sure that you have good rapport with those you work and live with. Practice the following skills and check off the ones you try in real life situations. Tomorrow is reflecting day so try and practice as many of these as you can.

Identify rapport-establishing phrases, and questions	
Use a style that is sympathetic and interested when you speak with others	
Identify suitable empathetic information-gathering questions	
Use sympathetic phrases and tone	
Listen for the natural empathy and sympathy based on building trust and rapport	
Take time to get to know people	
Do not belittle, diminish, reject, or ignore people	
Be receptive to others' cues, particularly the non-verbal ones such as facial expressions	
Try to relate with others	

Friday – Lesson #5 – Reflect

You made it! It is Friday and you have had the opportunity to practice a variety of skills that will assist you in your quest to become have more empathy and become an excellent Servant Leader. Take this day to reflect on Lessons #1 - #5 and use this time to write down some thoughts on which lessons you feel were hard and lessons you feel were easy.

Realize that empathizing is hard work	
Recognize your own biases	
Develop an appetite for learning more about your co-workers and family	
Prepare to empathize by having an open mind and a positive mental attitude	
Inspire good feelings through pleasant social interactions	
Reflect on people who are models of empathy, such as Mother Teres and Mahatma Gandhi	
Use your emotional intelligence to decide what to do when you feel empathy and what to do when someone else's moods are affecting you too much	
Reflect on your journaling	

Journal

Chapter 3

Healing-Can You Heal a Broken Spirit?

Week 3 – Healing

Don't you wish you could help those with a broken spirit? Well, you can. Healing…to help make whole. The search for wholeness is something shared by the Servant Leader and the led. Learning to heal is a powerful force for transformation and integration in the workplace and in the home. One of the greatest strengths of Servant Leadership is the potential for healing one's self and others. Servant leaders recognize that they have an opportunity to help those who have broken spirits and those who are suffering. What a powerful concept! You and I have the ability to help heal a person and make him/her whole.

A Servant Leader recognizes that people's work lives and personal lives are integrated and related and taps into both of those areas of a person. If our ability to perform well is missing in one area of life, it will affect our ability to perform well in the other areas of our lives. For example, if a person is dealing with a personal problem, it will affect how that person performs his/her job. The two worlds are related, even if we wish they weren't. A leader must be willing and able to recognize that others are able to perform better at work because of (not apart from) their activities and relationships outside the work environment. The healing characteristic of Servant Leadership recognizes that employees have many different areas that must work together for them to be successful in one area.

In *"The Servant as Leader,"* Greenleaf writes, "There is something subtle communicated to one who is being served and led if, implicit in the compact between the servant-leader and led is the understanding that the search for wholeness is something that they have." One way a Servant Leader heals is by creating an openness in which others feel comfortable to approach when something traumatic happens. Greenleaf went on to explain that human beings are in search of wholeness. He said, "that the servant-leader has an opportunity to contribute to the completeness of others by serving as a healing force between them." Unfortunately, we work and live with many people who are broken in spirit in today's world. Thankfully, the Servant Leader has developed the gift of healing those spirits.

Servant leaders are people who others want to go to when something eventful happens in their lives. These leaders have developed an astute appreciation for the emotional health and spirit of others and are good at facilitating the healing process. The ability to create an environment that encourages emotional mending is very important for those who want to become great Servant Leaders.

Monday – Lesson #1 –Create Self-Awareness

Healing is one of the most awesome characteristics of a Servant Leader. Imagine having the ability to heal oneself and others. Remember that one way to determine how effective a leader is, is to look at the followers. Are the followers happy, have they grown professionally, and have they grown personally while under the leadership of you? But, do you REALLY know yourself? It is the beginning of a new week and the beginning of our exercise on Healing. As you go about your day today, you will practice exercises that will help you get to know yourself better. In order to help others, you must first know how to help yourself. As you practice the art of healing, use the following as a checklist. At the end of the day, place a check mark next to each item that you completed.

Work on self-awareness – recognize and write down your own needs	
Reflect on your personal and professional goals – are you close to accomplishing some of them?	
Are you allowing and helping others to grow?	
Talk to others about their opinion of you as a person and as a leader	
Be prepared to listen to others' opinion of you with an open mind and an open heart	
Take notes and formulate a plan to improve	
How do other people feel about you	
Are you happy with yourself self image?	
Are you living a healthy life?	
Do you exercise regularly?	
Think before you act/speak	

Tuesday – Lesson #2 – Cultivate Compassion

I promise that yesterday was the hardest day of this week's lessons. Hearing what others think of you and receiving them openly is not an easy task. Today, you will work on cultivating compassion for others. As you did yesterday, please take the time at the end of the day today to reflect on your experiences and place a check mark on the following items that you practiced. As a reminder, at the end of the week, you will review all the strategies you practiced this week in order to develop your healing skills.

Seize opportunities today to model sympathetic feelings for other people	
In your journal, list the things you have in common with your coworkers	
In your journal, list the things you like about your family and friends	
Invite a coworker to lunch (preferably one you have NOT gotten to know well)	
Identify similarities between yourself and others	
Research opportunities to contribute to a worthy cause	
Ask about a coworker's family members	
Practice your listening skills (Week #1)	
Practice your empathy skills (Week #2)	
Do not belittle, diminish, reject, or ignore people	
No sarcasm	
Research problems around the world, learn more	
No putdowns	

Wednesday – Lesson #3 –Keep Your Emotions Under Control

Today, you will try to keep your emotions under control. It is much easier said than done, but I know how much you want to improve your leadership skills. We can all be a little "hot headed" at times and overreact to situations. Try these activities and see if they help you keep your emotions in check. As usual, place a check mark next to the items that you practiced today then at the end of the week you will reflect on what you learned and what you experienced.

Keep your emotions under control by using active listening skills	
Think before you act	
Set up your workspace to encourage relaxation	
Listen to calming music	
Surround yourself with people who are generally positive and thankful	
Read an uplifting article or book	
If you like flowers, have some fresh flowers on your desk as a quick pick me up	

Thursday – Lesson #4 –Perform Random Acts of Kindness

Today's lesson is on how to perform some random acts of kindness. I think you will be surprised at how good it makes you feel to do something for someone else…and not necessarily take any credit for it. To be a leader who serves, you must be able to help someone feel better. Practice the following skills and check off the ones you try in real life situations. Tomorrow is reflecting day so try and practice as many of these as you can.

When ordering in a drive thru, pay for the person's order behind you in the line	
Help someone carry their groceries to the car	
Give a little extra tip to the counter person at the coffee shop	
Leave a bottled water in the mailbox for the mailman	
Deliver a treat (like a Starbucks) to an elderly person…just make sure they can have sugar	
Randomly smile to strangers you come across during your work day	
Open the door for someone	
Make an anonymous donation to a charity of your choice	
In your journal, write about your feelings after performing some random acts of kindness	

Friday – Lesson #5 – Develop Your Emotional Intelligence

You made it! It is Friday and you have had the opportunity to practice a variety of skills that will assist you in your quest to become have more empathy and become an excellent Servant Leader. All this week you have been working on lessons that strengthen your Emotional Intelligence. Take this day to reflect on Lessons #1 - #5 and use this time to write down some comments on which lessons you feel were hard and lessons you feel were easy.

Realize that healing is hard work	
Recognize your own biases	
Develop an appetite for learning more about your co-workers	
Prepare to empathize by having an open mind and a positive mental attitude	
Inspire good feels through pleasant social interactions	
Use your emotional intelligence to decide what to do when you feel empathy and what to do when someone else's moods are affecting you too much	
Have an open mind and positive attitude	

Journal

Chapter 4

Awareness-Do You Walk the Talk?

Week 4 – Awareness

The leader has a general awareness but the servant leader has a unique self awareness. A person can develop awareness through self-reflection, listening to what others tell us about ourselves, being continually open to learning, and making the connection from what we know and believe to what we say or do. This is often referred to "walking your talk." Do you do what you say to do? Do you ask others to do what you would never do?

We must find every possible way to listen to put ourselves in the shoes of others. In today's schools, teachers struggle with a challenging student. If someone in the outer world is trying to tell us something important and we ignore his or her presence, the person either gives up and stops speaking or becomes more and more violent in attempting to get our attention.

"If the doors of perception were cleansed, everything will appear to man as it is, infinite." Most of us move about with very narrow perception. Awareness is not a giver of solace.. it is the opposite. It is a disturber and an awakener. Able leaders are usually sharply awake and reasonably disturbed. They are not seekers after solace. They have their own inner serenity.

General awareness, especially self awareness, strengthens the servant leader. Awareness also aids one in understanding issues involving ethics and values. It lends itself to being able to view most situations from a more integrated, holistic position.

Most leaders have a general awareness, but do you have the unique self-awareness that allows you to view most situations more holistically? It is essential that we learn how to make the connection between what we know and believe to what we say or do in order to lead effectively. I'm sure you have heard people say, if only "he/she would walk the talk." "Leaders and managers say they want change and improvement, but their actions do not match their words." And, I'm sure you have heard leaders and parents say, "just do what I say, not what I do." Do you do what you say? Do you ask others to do what you would never do? Once you find out something is not right, guess what....you have the responsibility to fix it. The solution to the problem then applies to you as well. Let me give you an example. You go to work and you notice that one of your employees is parking in the Handicapped parking slot right next to the front door. When you enter the office, you meet with that employee and tell him/her that they should refrain from parking in that slot unless they have a permit to do so. The employee states that she was in a hurry and was just running in the office to grab a file before heading to a meeting. You follow up with an email to everyone in the department reminding them that the Handicapped parking slot is reserved for those with an appropriate permit to park there. You direct them all to not use that slot unless they have the permit to do so. Fast forward the time and you find yourself in a position where you are in a hurry to meet with your boss but you need to pick up some paperwork at the office. There are no parking slots available except (you guessed it) the Handicapped one by the front door. You know it will only take 3 seconds to go in the office, get the paperwork, and return to the car. You don't think anyone will see you park there. What do you do? Well, I bet you know the answer, but still what do you do? A person who has refined his/her awareness skill is able to look at this situation holistically and will know that parking in that slot is not an option.

However, a person that is lacking in awareness will never address the problem from the very beginning with the employee parking there. Many times people will bury their heads in the sand (so to speak) just so they can claim they were not aware of a problem. Again, if you are aware...you have to do something about it and you just might not find that your solution to the problem is convenient for you.

According to Robert Greenleaf, "awareness is not a giver of solace. It is a disturber and an awakener." Servant Leaders are usually both acutely aware and somewhat disturbed. Because we all deal with issues of ethics and morality, we need to work on our ability to be aware and to do what we ask of others. If you work in an organization, you've heard the complaint that many times the leader's actions are contradictory to the change he/she is requiring of others. The power to change your organization's environment and culture is yours. Start here to learn how to walk your talk. I promise, it's the shortest journey to transform the work and home environment we all so desire.

Monday – Lesson #1 – Champion Others

Awareness is one more step toward becoming a more effective Servant Leader. The more aware you are as a leader, the more you will find what needs to be done. As you practice the skill of awareness, use the following as a checklist. At the end of the day, place a check mark next to each item that you completed. At the end of the week, you will reflect on all the steps you took to promote your awareness skills.

Show support for a colleague's idea in a meeting	
Share useful information with a coworker in another part of the company who otherwise wouldn't have received it	
Pitch in to help a teammate finish a presentation or prepare for it	
Be sincere	
Look for opportunities to be a good person	
Give first, receive later	
Lend a hand	
Believe in your organization	
Be willing to accept a certain amount of risk in allowing colleagues to try new strategies	
Celebrate small failures as a learning experience	
Personally congratulate someone for a great idea by writing a personal, hand written note of thanks	

Tuesday – Lesson #2 – Model The Behavior You Want to See in Others

We have talked a lot about seeking the positive in previous chapters. In order to be an effective Servant Leader, you can not let yourself fall prey to the negative minds of others. Nor can you let yourself instruct others to do that which you will not. So, today you will practice seeking the positive and modeling the behavior you want to see in others. Remember, it is difficult to break old habits. The only way we can change our behaviors is practice, practice, and practice yet again. As you did yesterday, please take the time at the end of the day today to reflect on your experiences today and place a check mark on the following items that you practiced. As a reminder, at the end of the week, you will review all the strategies you practiced this week in order to develop your awareness skills.

Identify the positive traits in another person	
Compliment the person on the positive identified trait	
Act as if you are part of the team, not always the boss of it	
If you make a rule, follow it	
Be clear about expectations for yourself and others	
Treat all with respect	
Clearly articulate the values that will guide the work you do and guide the decisions you make	

Wednesday – Lesson #3 –Help People Achieve Goals that are Important to Them

Day three is a bit easier. Today, you will work on your awareness of how to help people achieve goals that are important to them. If you do not know about something that is an issue with one of your colleagues or with your business, make it a point to investigate and find out more. The following activities will help you as you become more aware of how you can help others reach their goals. As usual, place a check mark next to the items that you practiced today then at the end of the week you will reflect on what you learned and what you experienced.

Become familiar with your colleague's priorities, values, and stated positions	
Research and read daily	
Make sure your colleagues have set goals for themselves both personally and professionally	
Ask open questions (who, what, how, why, when) to get people to open up and share their feelings	
Never, ever cheat!	

Thursday – Lesson #4 –Follow Thru!!!

Today's lesson is on the necessity of follow thru. If you only learn one thing this week, please make it this. Once you follow thru on what you say you are going to do, then you will see trust begin to develop. To be a leader who serves, you must be honest and aware. Practice the following skills and check off the ones you try in real life situations. Tomorrow reflecting day so try and practice as many of these as you can.

Have answers to questions	
Ask questions when possible, rather than make statements	
Have supporting evidence in hardcopy	
Don't be afraid to say, "I don't know"	
Do what you say you are going to do	
Admit your weaknesses	
Don't make rash promises that you can't keep	
Read works in progress	
Experiment with prototypes	
Read ideas and comments on whiteboard around the organization	
Sit in on department/staff meetings	
Talk to people	

Friday – Lesson #5 – Use Communication Tools

Friday has finally arrived. You have had the opportunity to practice a variety of skills. Today you will culminate your week with the development of your biography. Take this day to reflect on Lessons #1 - #5 and use this time to write down some comments on which lessons you feel were hard and lessons you feel were easy.

Collect testimonials and recommendations and share them	
Prepare a two-line biography detailing your skills with a contact number	
Share your information with friends and colleagues	
Build support for your organization's big goal	
Focus your meetings on the big goal	
Communicate a commitment to ideas, innovation, and growth in those you work with and those you work for	
Create a visual roadmap to move the organization from the current culture to the new one	
Prepare a report of the big issues, problems, weaknesses, and opportunities that the organization/home faces	

Journal

Chapter 5

Persuasion-Do You Seek to Convince Others?

Week 5 – Persuasion

Characteristics number five of servant leadership is persuasion. The Servant Leader primarily relies on making decisions within an organization based on persuasion rather than positional authority. In other words, you will never hear the Servant Leader say, "do it because I am the boss and I say to." The effective Servant Leader works toward convincing others rather than coercing compliance. This particular element offers one of the clearest distinctions between the traditional authoritarian model and the concept of servant leadership. The technique of convincing rather than coercing is one of the most effective ways a Servant Leader can build consensus within groups.

The Servant Leader has learned that it just doesn't pay off to raise a big storm about an issue or start a protest movement. The Servant Leader uses a method of gentle but clear and persistent persuasion. Leadership by persuasion has the virtue of change by convincement rather than coercion. Its advantages are enormous since great things get done one action at a time.

Transparent, fair, and consistent action by leaders may invite and persuade others to participate in the organization's community. Persuasion is formed when a feeling of rightness is obtained. Therefore, persuasion is ultimately about relationships. The more skills you have, the more able you will be to bring others to your side when you want their support. The good news is, you do not need to be a slick salesperson to be persuasive. A Servant Leader simply is able to see things clearly from other people's perspectives.

Effective Servant Leaders who are great persuaders don't ask themselves, "who can help me?" but instead ask, "whom can I help?" There are some basic techniques that can help you develop your persuasive skills. Try out the following tips and check off the ones you use each day. At the end of the week, you will reflect on your journey through the persuasion skill.

Monday – Lesson #1 – Create Transparency

It is the beginning of a new week and the beginning of our exercise to become more persuasive. Persuasion is one more step toward becoming a more effective Servant Leader. As you go about your day today, be conscious of how transparent your position is. Transparency is about being open, honest, and accountable. It's about responsibility. People are listening to you and making evaluations and decisions about what you say and what you do. So, you must take responsibility for the messages you send to others. As you practice the art of persuasive, use the following as a checklist. After doing some of these activities, you will see that transparency is nothing more than telling the truth. However, sometimes tell the truth is hard because we don't like to let people down or admit mistakes. But, embracing transparency will help you to be more open, honest, and accountable and connect better with others. At the end of the day, place a check mark next to each item that you completed. At the end of the week, you will reflect on all the steps you took to promote your empathy skills.

Talk about what you know	
Make a list of go-to people that specialize in areas that you don't know so much about	
Have an opinion and stay open to other views all at the same time	
Be responsible for the information that you share	
When you give your opinion, think through the implications	
Be truthful	
Make public all pertinent details	
Be timely and responsive	
Think community	
Know your audience	

Tuesday – Lesson #2 – Practice Fairness

O.k., Day 2 is ahead and you have now had some practice with transparency. Now, you need to practice focusing on the other person's positive attributes. Fairness occurs when the leader lives up to a promise made to several people. A great Servant Leader makes decisions that are fair. In addition, the leader must effectively communicate to others so that they fully understand the contexts of the decisions being made. Otherwise, others are likely to only see a part of the situation and may feel like the decision was unfair. As you did yesterday, please take the time at the end of the day today to reflect on your experiences and place a check mark on the following items that you practiced. If you want to be a better leader, focusing on fairness is a good place to start. Here are some things to try:

Always give people the credit they deserve	
Clearly communicate with others	
Listen to others	
Ensure that rules and policies are followed by all	
Maintain privacy and respect	
Practice what you preach	
Be open and honest about the reasons behind your decisions	
Create processes that allow people to understand how decisions are made	
Listen to both sides of the story	
Make sure you allow everyone a chance to have their voices heard	

Wednesday – Lesson #3 – Develop Consistency

Day three and you are getting the hang of things. You have practiced transparency and fairness. In addition to these skills, in order to be persuasive, you must be able to be consistent. To many people, the worst kind of leader is not one who is mean, strict, or demanding. People can adjust to just about any kind of leadership style, as long as they know what to expect. It is when a leader's behaviors and decisions differ from day to day that people find difficult to follow. People also have difficulty performing their tasks when they are working with a leader who treats people differently based on his/her mood at that moment. The most effective Servant Leaders must maintain a strong set of values, lead by example, and effectively communicate to others. How do you stay consistent? The following are a few tips to follow today. As usual, place a check mark next to the items that you practiced today then at the end of the week you will reflect on what you learned and what you experienced.

Use a calendar of planner	
Be accountable to someone	
Identify your core set of values	
Give yourself tangible reminders	
Practice patience	
Expect challenge	
Make the commitment	
Develop a system of renewal	
Stick to the basics	
Lead by example	

Thursday – Lesson #4 –Build Consensus

Today's lesson is on how to build consensus within your organization and/or your home. To be a leader who serves, you must be persuasive and be able to build a consensus. The word consensus comes from the Latin root meaning, "shared thought." However, consensus does not mean that you will attain complete agreement. It does, however, mean that it will involve seeking a decision with which everyone is reasonably comfortable. In order to accomplish this, everyone will need a fair opportunity to share their opinions. Consensus building resolves conflict and creates the energy necessary for people working on a common goal. Practice the following skills and check off the ones you try in real life situations. Tomorrow reflecting day so try and practice as many of these as you can.

Structure discussions so they remain focused	
List the issues on paper	
Listen to the opinions of others	
Get conflict out in the open	
Recognize and value differing viewpoints	
Keep asking questions	
Keep listing	
Reduce the long list using agreement	
Carefully discuss the remaining solutions	
Take a vote and rate the winning solutions	
Discuss the areas of disagreement further	
Vote again	
Discuss outcome – allowing everyone to be heard	
Ask, "Can everyone support the decision?"	

Friday – Lesson #5 – Create Relationships

You made it! It is Friday and you have had the opportunity to practice a variety of skills. As is often the case with persuasion, what you do first matters. One key component to being persuasive is the strength of your relationships with those you work and live with. Successful Servant Leaders have the ability to develop relationships that last. In today's economic environment, we all have to build successful work relationships and interact with people in a positive way in order to achieve our goals. Now, discover the ways in which you can build your basic skills that are critical to creating a solid relationship.

Balance giving and receiving	
Speak a little less, listen a little more	
Avoid gossip	
Practice forgiveness	
Know when to keep quiet	
Be trustworthy	
Set realistic goals and expectations	
Remain positive	
Communicate better	
Resolve conflict	
Accept difference in others	
Compliment others on a job well done	
Be supportive	
Encourage others	

Journal

Chapter 6

Conceptualization – Do You Dream Great Dreams?

Week 6 – Conceptualization

Conceptualization is the ability to nurture others to dream great dreams. The servant leader seeks to nurture the ability to dream great dreams in him/her as well as those of others. The ability to conceptualize allows Servant Leaders to create the vision in which to lead their organizations effectively towards a goal. Servant Leaders need to have the ability to see the whole picture. In addition, the Servant Leader needs to state and adjust goals, evaluate, analyze, and foresee problems before they actually occur. Servant Leadership, as it relates to stepping ahead to show the way, is more conceptual than operating. The people who can conceptualize are those who have refined skills in persuasion and relationship building.

The ability to look at a problem or an organization from a conceptualizing standpoint requires the leader to go beyond the day to day realities. For many leaders this is a characteristic that requires discipline and practice. Servant Leaders are called to seek a unique balance between conceptual thinking and a day to day focused approach by seeing what may be coming in the future while, at the same time, keeping up with the day to day activities of the organization.

Conceptualization is a process of thinking and organizing ideas. This process begins with the learning of facts and progresses to concepts that contribute to the development of theory. The Servant Leader must be able to set goals that consider future possibilities. In order to fully develop the skill of conceptualization, the Servant Leader must remain positive and realistic all at the same time. That takes some skill. It is easy for us to create outrageous goals, but are we ever really going to achieve them? It is also easy for us to dream small and make simple goals that we can achieve immediately. Those short term goals are good but we effective leaders are able to make long term goals that are difficult but not impossible to achieve. In order to set this type of goal, the leader must be able to use a variety of skills. This week, we will work toward developing all the necessary skills to become a great Servant Leader who can conceptualize.

Monday – Lesson #1 – Set Goals

We are now beginning Week 6 and the beginning of our exercise to improve our efforts at Conceptualization. Unlike the other skills, conceptualization is a bit harder to see. However, this guide will provide you some activities that will allow you to develop this difficult skill even further. Today, you will be thinking about how you set personal and professional goals for yourself and how you encourage others to set goals. Goal setting is a powerful process for turning your vision into reality. The process of setting goals helps us choose what is important to us. Achieving our goals can be incredibly motivating and can build self-confidence. At the end of the day, place a check mark next to each item that you completed. At the end of the week, you will reflect on all the steps you took to promote your conceptualization skills.

Set personal and professional goals	
Create the "big pictures" of what you want to do with your life	
Establish targets for reaching your goals	
State each goal in a positive statement	
Be precise by listing dates by which you want to have achieved the goal	
Set priorities	
Write the goals on paper	
Keep the goals small	
Set realistic goals	
Motivate yourself	
Don't underestimate yourself	
Stop procrastinating!	
Start with what you enjoy then work toward what is harder for you	

Tuesday – Lesson #2 – Get Organized

O.k., Day 2 is ahead and you have now had some practice with goal setting. Now, lets meet those goals by getting ourselves organized. We are our own worst enemies when it comes to getting organized. We tend to convince ourselves that we need things that we haven't used in five years. The Servant Leader is organized to make his/her life more functional and efficient. Use the following tips to help you develop an organizational system that works for you. As a reminder, at the end of the week, you will review all the strategies you practiced this week in order to develop your conceptualization skills.

Set up a filing system	
Color code your files	
Use a calendar and planner	
Set up reminders for yourself	
Write a to-do list	
Tackle unwanted projects first	
Finish a task before beginning another	
Manage your time	
Delegate tasks	
Open your mail everyday	
Use voice mail to assist with prioritizing calls	
Reduce clutter	
Organize files by priority	
Set up weekly appointments for things such as exercise and meal planning	
Reserve the computer desktop for files you use every day	
Create computer folders for documents	

If you are a frequent traveler, have a bag packed with traveling necessities	
Lay out your clothes the night before	

Wednesday – Lesson #3 – Analyze the Situation

Today's lesson is on analyzing the situation. Please make sure you document your analysis in your notes. As usual, place a check mark next to the items that you practiced today then at the end of the week you will reflect on what you learned and what you experienced.

Analyze the followers	
Collect information concerning the followers such as their duties and responsibilities on and off the job	
Formulate goals and objectives	
Communicate the core values of the organization	
Look at the history of the situation	
Prepare a SWOT analysis by listing the Strengths, Weaknesses, Opportunities, and Threats	
Examine the organization's strategy	
Make recommendations	

Thursday – Lesson #4 –Monitor Progress

Today's lesson builds on the analysis you made yesterday. Once you have analyzed the situation and made recommendations, you will need to monitor the progress. Once everyone in the organization knows what they need to do, there needs to be some monitoring in order to know that it is being done. Projects can become difficult to manage and a bit unorganized without some sort of monitoring. Monitoring should be based on the goals and timelines established. Practice the following skills and check off the ones you try in real life situations. Tomorrow reflecting day so try and practice as many of these as you can.

Choose appropriate materials for the followers comfort and familiarity with the organization.	
Schedule periodic check-up meetings	
Review data	
Fine-tune the plan	
Get help from others	
Assess rate of progress to the plan	
Identify opportunities for improvement	
Check off tasks as they are being successfully completed	
Conduct site visits	
Provide feedback	

Friday – Lesson #5 – Plan and Evaluate

You made it! It is Friday and you have had the opportunity to practice a variety of skills. Program evaluation is carefully collecting information in order to make necessary decisions and recommendations. Evaluations can identify program strengths and weakness that will lead to improved programs. Evaluations can also verify to the Servant Leader that what you are doing is what you think you are doing. It can verify if programs are being implemented as planned.

Review the goals	
Evaluate your efforts in order to improve and promote the effectiveness	
Use questionnaires, surveys, interviews, etc.	
Tabulate information for ease with sharing	
Read all data carefully	
Organize data	
Identify patterns with the responses	
Record conclusions and make recommendations	
Conduct planning meetings	
Determine if followers are growing both personally and professionally	
Conduct a Needs Assessment	
Prepare a Cost/Benefit Analysis	
Determine the effectiveness of the plan	

Journal

Chapter 7

Foresight – Do You Have an Intuitive Mind?

Week 7 – Foresight

To have foresight means to have the ability to understand lessons from the past. A Servant Leader must have the ability to foresee or know the likely outcome of a given situation. Hopefully, you are not just guessing your way through life and hoping for the best. Leaders can develop the skill of foresight through their experiences on the job and in life. All of us have foresight; we just need to develop the skill of recognizing it in order to solve problems that are creative, emotional, intellectual, or practical.

Robert Greenleaf says, "it is a better than an average guess about what is going to happen." He says, "it is the lead that a leader has." He goes on to state: "foresight is seen as a wholly rational process, the product of a constantly running internal computer that deals with intersecting series and random inputs and is vastly more complicated than anything technology has yet produced."

Foresight means looking at what is happening right now and comparing it to has happened in the past and the result that came of it. At the same time, the leader has to project what will happen in the future. It is essential that leaders develop this skill as it has the power to transform organizations and lives.

A forward-looking person has the ability to analyze any situation with the foresight necessary to make decisions. Foresight is a characteristic that enables the Servant Leader to understand the lessons from the past, the realities of the present, and the likely consequence of a decision for the future. To get really good at foresight, one must develop the intuitive mind. There are many ways in which you can develop your skill of foresight. Some may work for you and some may not. The key is to try as many of them as you can in order to find the ones you are more comfortable with.

Follow some of the suggestions in this week's lesson and you will begin to develop your intuitive mind to enhance your ability to use the skill of foresight.

Monday – Lesson #1 – Focus on the Issue

It is the beginning of a new week and we begin today learning and practicing the concept of foresight. Foresight is an important step in becoming an effective servant leader. As you go about your day today, be conscious of how you pay special attention to the issue at hand. As you practice the art of foresight, use the following as a checklist. After doing some of these activities, you will feel better able to prepare for what comes tomorrow. At the end of the day, place a check mark next to each item that you completed. At the end of the week, you will reflect on all the steps you took to promote your empathy skills.

Identify the issue(s)	
Prioritize the issues	
Review the organization's mission	
Eliminate any issues that are not related to your organization's mission and vision	
Take one thing at a time	
Do not procrastinate	
Make a to-do list	
Ask for help	
Provide a more organized work environment	
Use noise cancellation devices, if necessary	
Create solutions that will provide for a better environment in which to work	
Nurture yourself	
Provide positive feedback	
Take a deep breath, smile, and exhale	
Balance your mental and emotional mind	

Tuesday – Lesson #2 – Scan Your Environment

Now it is time to practice scanning your environment to help you develop more foresight. As you did yesterday, please take the time at the end of the day today to reflect on your experiences and place a check mark on the following items that you practiced. As a reminder, at the end of the week, you will review all the strategies you practiced this week in order to develop your persuasion skills.

Look internally and externally at your organization to identify what is on the horizon that may impact the issues you identified yesterday	
Decide if change is societal, technological, economical, environmental, and/or political	
Identify the driving forces behind the change	
Try to determine the POSSIBLE future	
Try to determine the PROBABLE future	
Try to determine the PREFERRED future	
List all the forces driving change	
Communicate effectively with others	
Participate in planning and making change	
Support others	
Listen more	
Negotiate to match goals of the members to the goals of the organization	

Wednesday – Lesson #3 – Set the Vision

Today is Day Three and you are beginning to get the hang of foresight. There are at least five benefits for taking time to identify alternative futures. First, you are less likely to be surprised by the future. Second, your organization will be better prepared to successfully deal with the future. Third, it encourages an organization to think about current assumptions. Fourth, it allows the organization to conduct an "if…then" analysis. Finally, fifth, the organization can plan and act differently now. Today, you will work on setting the vision. Many opportunities will present themselves; however, when deciding where the organization is going, you can be sure of what activities are right and what are wrong. You need to ensure that the opportunities you take make great use of the organization's skills. A vision is a catalyst that aligns people in activities across the organization. In addition, a vision will facilitate goal setting and planning. A vision will also unleash energy as it embodies the organization's core values. As usual, place a check mark next to the items that you practiced today then at the end of the week you will reflect on what you learned and what you experienced.

Envision the future of your organization	
Jot down the images that come to mind	
Tell people what your specific vision is	
Describe what your organization will look like six months from now	
Review your core values	
Create a clear and compelling vision statement	

Thursday – Lesson #4 –Develop the Plan

Now that you have envisioned the future and set the vision, today's lesson will help you develop a plan that will set that vision in motion and lead and continue to help you develop your foresight skill. It is important that the foresight process connects the preferred future with the organization as it is today. It is a way of saying, "Here is where we are and here is where we want to be in the future. And, this plan is how we are going to get there." To be a leader who serves, you must be able to vision and plan. Practice the following skills and check off the ones you try in real life situations. Tomorrow is reflecting day so try and practice as many of these as you can.

Focus your attention back to the present	
Consider the range of possible futures – what is the best for the organization?	
Develop specific goals and strategies to move the organization in the direction of the desired future	
Organize and implement a planning development session	
Act as a facilitator	
Include others in formulating the plan	
Define the purpose	
List the Critical Success Factors	
Prioritize and develop and implementation schedule	
Use the finished plan as an operational tool to define the organization's current status and future possibilities	

Friday – Lesson #5 –Put the Plan into Action

It is Friday and you have had the opportunity to practice a variety of skills this week. The last step to developing your foresight is to implement the plan. Like any planning process, communication is essential to involving the people who will be vital to the successful implementation of the plan. The final step does not mean that the organization is done with the plan. Instead, foresight needs to continue to be used in order to identify further changes in the environment and feed that information back into the organization. As you can tell by now, foresight requires a willingness to learn, a certain amount of flexibility, humbleness, and balance. Take this day to reflect on Lessons #1 - #5 and use this time to write down some comments on which lessons you feel were hard and lessons you feel were easy.

Define what processes will be changed	
Determine how progress with the plan will be evaluated	
Indicate who will be responsible for which strategies	
Check off items on your to-do list as they are completed	
Monitor the implementation of the plan	
Review and evaluate the plan on an annual basis	
Create new opportunities based on evaluations	

Journal

Chapter 8

Stewardship- Are You a Good Steward?

Week 8 - Stewardship

How do we care for those things that matter most? Stewardship is described as holding something in trust for another. We all are stewards of those around us. We are stewards of our family, our colleagues, our friends, and our organizations. The art of Servant Leadership requires us to be stewards not only in terms of assets and legacies, but also of momentum, effectiveness, civility, and values.

Most people struggle with what stewardship actually means. To some, it means budgeting and saving money. To others it means developing financial independence. However, stewardship simply means holding something in trust for another. All members of an institution or organization should play significant roles in holding their institutions in trust. The Servant Leader cares for the well being of the institution by serving the needs of others in the institution for the greater good of society. The Servant Leader is also responsible for properly utilizing and developing the resources needed in the organization (including the people). An effective Servant Leader, while using the skill of stewardship, serves others while staying focused on achieving the organization's goals. These leaders use collaboration, trust, and empathy in order to better serve others with the objective of enhancing the growth of those within the organization and increase teamwork and personal involvement.

The Servant Leader understands and embraces the need to make a contribution to society. Through service, these leaders have the capacity to be a steward of the public good. Stewardship involves the leader's personal responsibility to manage her/his life and affairs with proper regard for the rights of other people and for the common welfare of the organization and society. Effective Servant Leaders are confident, courageous, and competent and know how to be good stewards of what they have been given. Stewardship describes a commitment to serving the needs of others utilizing the use of openness and persuasion, rather than control.

You are invited to begin a new journey to stewardship by practicing the tips below this week. We should all be asking ourselves what our role is in making the changes necessary to improve our organizations and ourselves.

Monday – Lesson #1 –Work Smart

It is the beginning of a new week and the beginning of our exercise to become a more effective steward. Do you end the day wishing for more hours? If so, there are ways to get more from your day without having to need more hours. At the end of the day, place a check mark next to each item that you completed. At the end of the week, you will reflect on all the steps you took to promote your stewardship skills.

Research opportunities for volunteers to contribute to your organization	
Treat employees like adults	
Write less, talk more	
Take time to think	
Begin meetings on time	
Do not have meetings that last longer than two hours	
Teach employees the importance of balancing work and home responsibilities	
Organize work spaces within your organization	
Create and keep a schedule	
Keep all telephone calls short and on topic	
Have separate email accounts for work and personal	
Set time limits on how long you have to work on a specific task	
Keep your favorite internet sites bookmarked	
Organize your day to include regular breaks and time to eat	
Keep your desk clear from clutter	

<u>Tuesday – Lesson #2 –Explore nontraditional funding</u>

O.k., Day 2 is ahead and you have now had some practice with working smarter as you become a more effective steward and Servant Leader. Today, we are looking at ways to explore nontraditional funding. As a reminder, at the end of the week, you will review all the strategies you practiced this week in order to develop your stewardship skills.

Develop a relationships with your suppliers

Attend as many networking events as possible

Plan cause oriented events

Develop partnerships with service clubs

Seek grant opportunities

Develop partnerships with foundations

Wednesday – Lesson #3 – Exploit Technology

Exploit technology? Yes, I mean exploit it. We live in a new technological world and it is time for us all to use the technology available. Technology can be intimidating but just look at an eight year old and you will see that if he/she can use the computer, there is no reason why we can't. Don't be afraid to ask those who use technology more than you. They are always willing to share what they know. The following tips will help you on your quest to exploit technology today.

Rethink your business model for the 21st century	
Explore transitioning to eBusiness	
Investigate the importance of intangible assets	
Integrate new technologies	
Explore redesigning business processes using the internet	
Attend technology training seminars	

Thursday – Lesson #4 –Save, Save, Save

Today's lesson is one of the hardest lessons in our economic environment. Yet, it is one of the most important. How do we balance financial responsibility with giving sacrificially? We must make the distinction between financial responsibility and financial foolishness. The following tips will help you look at your financial situation a little better.

Anticipate future needs and save for them	
Don't spend on short term indulgences with no thought of saving for upcoming needs or providing for the company's future	
Look for ways to save without reducing your giving	
Review your budget and look for ways to cut back	
Evaluation your spending patterns	

Friday – Lesson #5 – Give, Give, Give

You made it! It is Friday and you have had the opportunity to practice a variety of skills this week. Saving can be wise, but it can never substitute for giving. If ever we don't feel we can save and give, by all means we should give. In the truest sense, generous giving is not just compassionate, it is also responsible. The tips listed here will help you see how you can give. Check off the ones you have tried today then reflect on this entire week's lesson.

Clean out your offices and donate old furniture and supplies that are no longer used	
Give wisely	
Select a worthy cause that is directly related to your company's mission and vision	
Allow employees time to volunteer in the community	
Develop partnerships with local non-profit organizations	
Schedule time for yourself to volunteer at local schools, non profits, libraries, or community organizations	

Journal

Chapter 9

Growth of People – Are You Nurturing?

Week 9 – Growth of People

Growth can be personal or professional. It just isn't enough these days that organizations are providing their employees with paychecks and vacations. People have intrinsic value and expect that they will be fulfilled both personally and professionally at their job. The Servant Leader know this and is committed to the growth of people. The Servant Leader will devote himself/herself to serving the needs of the organization's members while developing the members to bring out the best in them. A true Servant Leader will develop the ability to nurture the personal, professional, and spiritual parts of those he/she works and lives with. Being interested in a person's growth will usually result in more respect, dedication, and loyalty. More importantly, it will develop a more productive, fulfilled, and effective contributor to the organization and society.

The Servant Leader is committed to the individual growth of others and will work intentionally to nurture them. We should be reminded that the signs of outstanding leadership can be seen in the followers. Are the followers reaching their potential? Are the followers learning? Are the followers serving? The Servant Leader actually serves as a follower who leads by modeling, teaching, and helping others to become better followers. This process creates leadership based on stewardship and service as opposed to a direct leadership based on rules and hierarchy.

Nurturing and educating others is an ongoing process that promotes growth in people and in organizations. Fostering leadership at many levels is one of the Servant Leader's main roles because the effective Servant Leader recognizes the responsibility to do everything possible to nurture the growth of employees and others. There is a firm belief that people have value as individuals as well as workers. Being committed to the growth of each individual within an institution will lead to the growth of the institution. In addition, a leader's own growth is facilitated by the growth of others.

A servant leader views leadership not as position or status, but as an opportunity to serve others, to develop them to their full potential. Greenleaf believed the final goal of servanthood was to help others become servants themselves so that society would benefit as well. In servant leadership, personal development is not limited to the followers, but the leader also benefits from the developmental process.

Monday – Lesson #1 – Motivate Your Staff

Personal growth is not one of those things that you can do and then forget about. Instead, it is an ideology that both the leader and the follower must agree to. Using this ideology, the leader becomes the example that will help to motivate others. Today, you will be practicing the skill of motivation in order to promote growth in people. In order to find out how effective of a leader you are, one must only look to the followers and see how much they have grown under your leadership. The following is a list of activities that you do today that will help you develop your motivation skills. After you try them, place a check mark in the box to the right.

Establish an Open Door Policy where anyone can meet with you to discuss issues	
Offer flex time to motivate employees to participate in growth activities	
Offer tuition reimbursement, if possible.	
Offer financial reward for improved job performance	
Make jobs assignments interesting and challenging	
Create a team	
Provide support for those trying to grow	
Praise even the smallest accomplishments	
Squash negative attitudes	
Create job opportunities that allow employees to be satisfied with their assignment	

Tuesday – Lesson #2 –Create Opportunities to Learn

In today's information-driven society, the organization that employs the best-informed people will be better prepared to compete. Personal growth is the catalyst that will allow an organization to compete and grow. The leader can have the biggest impact on whether or not the employees seek to grow. Opportunity is an environmental factor that the leader can create. Today, try and do some things that will promote opportunities to learn for your staff. In turn, these opportunities may contribute to the goal of nurturing growth in people.

Make written resources available to staff	
Encourage employees to use free time to read	
Sign up for mailing lists of organizations	
Encourage employees to attend college or universities	
Set the example by taking some courses	
Invite college representatives to your next staff meeting	
Organize book study groups	
Schedule seminars and classes in-house	

Wednesday – Lesson #3 – Set Goals

An important part of nurturing growth in others is helping your colleagues set goals for themselves. Goals represent our expectations, our hopes, and our dreams. When we create goals, we are predicting the future and setting our destiny. Think of setting goals as drawing a map. You will reach your goals if you first know exactly where you are and where you want to go. Goals direct our focus, so make them powerful. The following ideas will help you establish goals in your life as well as allowing you to help others set goals in their lives.

Make a finish line – then move it	
Set daily, weekly, and yearly goals	
Once a goal has been achieved, set a new one	
Make sure the goal is conceivable – you must be able to imagine it	
Create a goal that is believable because it relates to your core value system	
Set a goal that requires you to stretch	
Keep a copy of your written goals in sight so that you can refer to it daily	

<u>Thursday – Lesson #4 –Find the Silver Lining</u>

Personal growth is a journey, not a destination, and setbacks will happen. It is important to realize that the journey to your destination (or goal) will not always be easy. You will encounter bumps along the way to reaching your goals. Growing is all about putting one foot in front of the other with the objective of improving yourself every day. Today's lesson is about finding the silver lining. The following tips will help you accept that mistakes will happen, learn from them, and make sure not to repeat them. As a Servant Leader, you must know how to find the silver lining in any situation.

Realize and accept setbacks	
Help your staff learn from these setbacks	
Recognize that setbacks are opportunities to improve	
Look at setbacks as temporary situations	
Don't point fingers and blame others	
No excuses allowed!	
Try a new idea	
Don't apologize for taking a risk	
Keep an open mind	
Allow your emotions to stay in check – don't take things personally	
Find the positive	

Friday – Lesson #5 – Reflect

It is Friday and you have had the opportunity to practice a variety of skills. Take this day to reflect on Lessons #1 - #5 and use this time to write down some comments on which lessons you feel were hard and lessons you feel were easy. The process of reflection is an important component to developing your skill of nurturing.

Provide reflection time daily for your staff	
Reflection time should be focused on personal growth	
Review your goals and your timeline for accomplishing them	
Spend some time to record your feelings in your journal	

Journal

Chapter 10

Building Community- Do You Serve Others?

Week 10 – Building Community

Servant Leaders have a different way of looking at how people work together. These leaders create a community with a sense that all are part of a team working toward an agreed upon vision. A truly effective leader has learned how to serve and be served. Through this process of serving, the servant leader seeks to find a way of building community, resisting the temptation to just get the job done. True community can be created and the effective Servant Leader will encourage participation and build consensus. In addition, the Servant Leaders strives at creating a community of leaders through the generation of a shared vision. Using effective communication and partnerships, the leader will build a community that will contribute to the success of the organization. Servant Leaders intentionally work to build a community that works together and learns to serve.

Because Servant Leaders are best prepared to bring about large-scale and lasting change, these leaders listen closely to those they work and live with. Some ways to building community can include giving back to the through service; financially investing in the community; and caring about the community. Such simple steps are ways in which a leader can build the community in which he/she lives and works. Active participation in community life can promote happiness and fulfillment of both personal and professional goals. Volunteering in communities emphasizes the sense of belonging. This sense of belonging comes from a shared sense of purpose.

A Servant Leader will encourage and identify means for building community among those who he/she works and lives with. Additionally, the Servant Leader uses personal trust and respect to build bridges and do what is best for the followers and the organization. The effective leader will create community spirit by instilling pride in their organization. Servant Leadership suggests that true community can be built among those who work in business and other institutions.

The following tips are designed to further develop the skill of building community.

Monday – Lesson #1 – Communicate the Vision

Vision means being able to motivate the community with large, desired outcomes. Large outcomes require creating goals that attract followers. The vision must contain challenge, appeal to personal pride, and provide an opportunity to make a difference and realize the difference that is being made. Today, we will practice the skill of communicating the vision. In previous lessons, we have discussed the steps to creating the vision. Today, we need to make sure that we are effectively communicating that vision. Practice some of the activities listed below and place a check mark next to the ones you tried. Don't be afraid to experiment and take some risks. At the end of the week, you will see that your ability to build community has improved.

Clearly communicate the vision	
Position the vision by picturing success	
Be confident	
Ask yourself, "What will success be like and/or feel like?"	
Ask yourself, "How will others know what success is?"	
Get interested in those you work with	
Create a short, sharp, to the point vision statement	
Use storytelling techniques that help your vision come to life	
Compose and "elevator speech" that will communicate the vision statement in a clear, brief way	
Use multiple media (meetings, memos, emails, texts, lunches, etc.)	
Engage others in one-on-one conversations	
Identify key players, stakeholders, and supporters	
Communicate to external people with announcements and brochures	

Create metaphors, slogans, mottos, etc.	
Use visual aids and updates to keep everyone aware of the vision	
Back up your talk with actions and behaviors that support the vision	

Tuesday – Lesson #2 – Establish Commitment

Commitment can be a tricky concept because some people may assume that commitment means long hours and more work. However, when expectations are defined, commitment increases. Commitment is actually a critical factor in team success. The relationships developed from the commitment by the team members are essential to team success. Individuals and organizations that feel truly committed tend to have a strong sense of purpose and vision. People who feel engaged, involved, and energized tend to have a stronger commitment. Today, we will practice the skill of commitment. Don't forget to check off the items that you try today.

Define expectations	
Remove all doubt from the organization	
Provide support	
Establish an atmosphere of trust	
Encourage inclusion	
Choose your team members carefully	
Value all the team members	
Challenge your team with opportunities	
Recognize successful teams and projects	
Address immediate needs	

Wednesday – Lesson #3 – Establish Trust

Trust means confidence in and commitment to the organization's leadership and vision. When there is trust, team members are more willing to commit to the organization – even when going through difficult times. Trust is most effectively established when the Servant Leader communicates his/her commitment to the vision. Today. Day three of our lesson on Building Community, you will practice the skills that will promote more trust in your organization. Try them all and see what happens!

Make known your commitment to the vision	
List the unknowns	
Assess worst case scenarios and their survivability	
Research the unknowns	
Plan to share risks and rewards with colleagues	
Establish and maintain integrity	
Consider all employees as equal partners	
Do what is right – always!	
Act and speak consistently	
Do not withhold information	
Never lie	
Remain open-minded	

Thursday – Lesson #4 –Include Others

Today's lesson is on how to include others in the organization. Inclusion involves getting others to commit to the community effort of attaining agreed upon goals. In order to promote inclusion, a Servant Leader must assist those who are doubtful that they can achieve commitment to the vision of the organization. The following skills will help you practice inclusion in your organization. As you try each of them, place a checkmark in the box.

Communicate effectively with everyone	
Ask non-assumptive questions like, "What do you think?" and "Can you tell me what is happening with this report?"	
Invite real answers	
Listen, don't judge	
Demonstrate responsiveness by responding directly	
Create and environment in which others feel safe and confident	
Involve everyone	
Provide a range of activities based on needs and interests of others	
Hear and consider others' ideas	
Practice active listening	
Promote discussions with a variety of view points	

Friday – Lesson #5 – Reflect – Are You a "10?"

The final step in building community is to reflect on all the previous lessons and evaluate your skills using the following questionnaire. Answer the questions honestly. Wherever you find yourself answering "no" you may have discovered a goal for yourself. A balanced strategy for reaching your goal of being a more effective Servant Leader can be developed from this workbook. As Robert Greenleaf stated, "…each of us is intimately connected to the other, and in recognizing that connection, we are moved to greater service; to a more profound understanding, appreciation, and tolerance of one another; to an honest self-examination of our own attitudes and behavior; and to the building of community" (Greenleaf, 2003).

    Answer each question with "Yes/No"

Do people believe that you want to hear their ideas and value them?	
Do people believe that you will understand what is happening in their lives and how it affects them?	
Do people come to you when the chips are down or when something traumatic has happened in their lives?	
Do others believe that you have a strong awareness for what is going on?	
Do others follow your requests because they want to as opposed to because they "have to?"	
Do others communicate their ideas and vision for the organization when you are around?	
Do others have confidence in your ability to anticipate the future and its consequences?	
Do others believe you are preparing the organization to make a positive difference in the world?	
Do people believe that you are committed to helping them develop and grow?	

Do people feel a strong sense of community in the organization that you lead?

Journal

References

Barbuto, J.E. Jr., & Wheeler, D.W. (2007). *Becoming a servant leader: do you have what it takes?* University of Nebraska-Lincoln Extension, Institute of Agriculture and Natural Resources.

Greenleaf, R.K. (2003). *The servant-leader within: A transformative path.* Mahwah, NJ: Paulist Press.